THE SIXTIES IN PICTURES

James Lescott

THE SIXTIES IN
PICTURES

Bath · New York · Singapore · Hong Kong · Coogne · Delhi · Melbourne

This edition published in 2008

Parragon Books Ltd
Queen Street House
4 Queen Street
Bath, BA1 1HE

Created and produced by:
Endeavour London Ltd.
21-31 Woodfield Road
London W9 2BA

With great thanks to the team
at Endeavour London Ltd. –
Jennifer Jeffrey, Kate Pink,
Franziska Payer-Crockett and
Liz Ihre

Text © Parragon Books Ltd
2007

ISBN 978-1-4054-9523-3

Printed in China

All images courtesy of Getty
Images who is grateful to the
following photographers and
image libraries represented by
Getty Images for their kind
assistance.

20th Century Fox: 106-107;
Agence France Presse: 170-
171, 199, 203, 208, 232-233,
240-241; CBS Archives: cover;
Columbia Studios: 81, 136,
213; Eon Productions: 103,
137; FBI: 112; MGM Studios:
237; NASA: 62, 143, 245; Alan
Oxley: 38; Paramount
Pictures: 32, 54, 102, 212(b);
Roger Viollet : 111, 184(tr),
184(b), 185, 189; Time & Life
Pictures: frontispiece, 8, 14-
17, 19-20, 22-23, 26-31, 40-50,
53, 55-56, 59(b), 60(b), 61,
63-64, 69-74, 76, 82-85, 98-
101, 102(b), 103, 108-109, 110,
113-114, 116, 119(t), 120, 122,
131, 137, 141, 143, 151, 154-
158, 163, 167-169, 176-178,
180, 182-183, 186, 204-206,
211, 214-215, 218-219, 221,
223, 226, 228-229, 235, 237,
247-248(t), 249, 254; United
Artists: 80, 125; Warner
Brothers: 212(t)

Frontispiece
Amid the turmoil, the dreams of youth were in
full colour and psychedelically way-out in the
1960s. Two richly decorated lovers gaze out to
sea near Latana, Florida, June 1967.

Page 7
"The only chain that a man can stand, is the
chain of hand in hand..." Martin Luther King Jr
and his wife Coretta Scott King keep their eyes
on the prize as they march through the 1960s.

Contents

Introduction

For many, they will always be the Swinging Sixties, although that was not how they appeared to the millions embroiled in war and the struggle to survive in Southeast Asia, sub-Saharan Africa, or even the Deep South of the United States. While some strutted their youthful way past the flower-bedecked shop windows of the King's Road and Carnaby Street, others marched in purposeful dignity from Selma to Montgomery, or died in the dust at Sharpeville. Freedom in Chelsea meant the Pill: in Alabama and South Africa it meant the Vote.

It was not a dull age. There was a myriad new things to view and do. The mini crept up female legs: The Mini raced along new roads. Airliners swelled in size: package holidays shrank in price. The music industry had never had it so good: the movie industry had never been so racked with worry, as television extended its claws and doubled its ratings. The Beatles invaded America: the CIA invaded Cuba. Mick Jagger was sent to prison for three months, Nelson Mandela for life. One American became the first man to walk on the Moon, another American fell to earth in a U2 spy-plane. Popular risings were crushed in Prague and Paris. The Cultural Revolution swept through China. Rioting broke out in Watts, Detroit, Grosvenor Square, the Bogside, and points north, south, east, and west. A Six-Day War advanced Israel's borders in the Middle East. Heart transplants, microwave ovens, and skateboards all made their first appearance.

Violent death came to many of the movers and shakers throughout the world. Two Kennedys were gunned down. Martin Luther King Jr and Malcolm X, contrasting leaders of Black America, were assassinated. Henrik Verwoerd, architect of Apartheid, was stabbed to death. Suspicion and mystery still hangs over the death of Dag Hammarsköld, Secretary-General of the United Nations, in a plane crash. Patrice Lumumba was murdered in the Congo. Che Guevara was murdered in Bolivia by the reactionary forces that he had challenged all his brief life. Marilyn Monroe took an overdose. Jayne Mansfield crashed her car.

It was a swinging era, when the highs were very high, and the lows were as low as they always seem to be.

Although de Gaulle negotiated with the FLN (*Front de libération nationale*), the savage and dirty fighting between those seeking independence and right-wing colonialists continued in **Algeria**. (*Above*) French soldiers monitor an FLN demonstration in the Casbah, Algiers, 14 December 1960. (*Left*) Colonel Pierre Lagaillarde (on right), leader of the French rebel troops, prepares to surrender.

On the night of 29 February 1960, the Moroccan town of **Agadir** was hit by a violent earthquake which killed 12,000 people and injured another 12,000. (*Left*) Rescue workers lift one of the earthquake victims from the rubble.

(*Above*) To assist identification, a health inspector makes notes on bodies recovered from the ruins of the town. Most of the victims were then buried in pits of quicklime to prevent the spread of disease.

The **Sharpeville** massacre in South Africa shocked the world. On 23 March 1960 some 6,000 people assembled in Sharpeville to demonstrate against the Pass Laws. Without warning, police fired on the crowd, killing 69 and injuring 180. (*Above*) Dead and wounded lie in the streets. (*Left*) Police remove the body of a woman killed in the massacre.

Anti-segregation protest intensified
in America's Deep South. (*Left*) A group
of students from Nashville, Tennessee
take their lunch in jail following their
arrest for boycotting a lunch counter.
(*Above*) The proprietor of a lunch counter
surveys his empty diner, May 1960.

Cold War crisis. (*Left*) Gary Powers, whose **U-2 spy plane** was shot down over the USSR in May 1960. (*Above*) Debris from the plane is exhibited in Moscow. (*Right*) The main wreckage of the plane. Powers was imprisoned for two years before being exchanged for a Soviet spy.

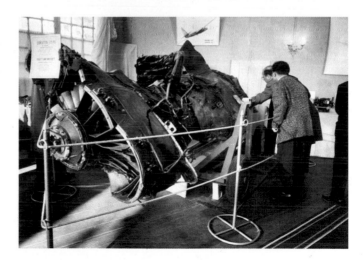

Trouble flared in the newly independent
Congo, with Belgian soldiers supporting their
government's attempt to separate the province
of Katanga from the rest of the country. (*Left*)
Swedish UN troops en route from Cairo to
Leopoldville, 20 July 1960. (*Above*) Philippe
Kanza (left) and André Mandi (centre) at a UN
Security Council session on the Congo.

The **Rome Olympics** were hailed as the biggest and best ever, though they were also the first at which the problem of drugs was identified. (*Right*) Spectators at the Stadio dei Marmi, Rome, 26 August 1960. (*Above*) The German sprinter Armin Harry gets off to a flying start in the Men's 100 Metres, 1 September 1960.

The star of the Rome Games was **Wilma Rudolph**, who won three gold medals. (*Left*) Rudolph wins the Women's 100 Metres, 1 September 1960. The American athlete **Ralph Boston** (*right*) set a new World Record in the Long Jump.

(*Left*) US fears increased when Soviet Prime Minister Nikita Krushchev (on right) and the new Cuban leader **Fidel Castro** met at the UN in New York in September 1960. (*Above*) There were, however, plenty of supporters of the Cuban revolution waiting to welcome Castro to New York.

After a spell in the political wilderness, the Democratic Party in the United States sensed new hope and the promise of a return to power in the 1960s. Their great hope was the charismatic John Kennedy, who they reckoned would give Nixon a run for his money. (*Above*) Frenzy and razzmatazz at the **Democratic Convention** in Los Angeles, 31 October 1960.

The Democrats were right to be optimistic.
Kennedy won the Presidential election by a narrow
margin. (*Above*) Kennedy (on left) and Richard
Nixon, rival candidates for President, meet in
October 1960. (*Right*) The newly-elected President,
with friends and family, delivers his victory speech
at Hyannisport, Massachusetts, November 1960.

Golden Years of the Great Game. Mickey
Mantle (*left*) relaxes after hitting two home
runs for the Yankees against the Pirates in
the **World Series**, 10 January 1960. On the
same day (*above*), students at the University
of Pittsburgh gaze down at faraway Forbes
Field and cheer on the Pirates.

The film sensation of 1960 was Alfred Hitchcock's **Psycho**. (*Left*) Janet Leigh, with Bernard Herrmann's screeching violins on the soundtrack, screams her way through the famous shower scene. (*Right*) Hitchcock holds a clapperboard on the *Psycho* set, 29 January 1960.

The political dust never settled on the Sharpeville Massacre. (*Left*) South African Prime Minister Hendrik Verwoerd and his wife leave Cape Town on 21 February 1961, on their way to the Commonwealth Prime Ministers Conference in London. Within a month **South Africa** was to leave the Commonwealth. (*Above*) South Africans demonstrate in Pretoria during a visit by the UN Secretary-General, 10 January 1961.

Science fiction became fact on 12 April
1961 when the Soviet cosmonaut, Major
Yuri Gagarin (*right*) became the first man
to travel in space, orbiting the earth in
the 4.7 ton spaceship *Vostok 1*. His flight
lasted 108 minutes and made Gagarin a
worldwide celebrity. (*Above*) London
office workers read of Gagarin's flight.

Backed by the US and masterminded by the
CIA, an army of mercenaries and Cuban exiles
attempted an invasion of Cuba on 14 April 1961.
The resulting shambles became known as the
Bay of Pigs invasion. (*Right*) Some 1,170
prisoners taken during the invasion are tried
at an open-air military court in Havana. (*Above*)
Fidel Castro at a press conference following
ransom negotiations for the prisoners in June
1961. They were eventually released in
exchange for $53 million in medical supplies.

The Civil Rights Campaign in
the southern United States
continued. (*Above*) Guarded by
two national guardsmen, Julia
Aaron and David Dennis sit with
25 other **Freedom Riders** on a
bus from Montgomery, Alabama
to Jackson, Mississippi, May 1961.

Montgomery had been the scene of
the early bus boycotts in the 1950s and
was still the centre of Civil Action. As
the campaign grew, the white backlash
became more violent, with 1,000 whites
attacking the Freedom Riders. (*Above*)
White opponents of integration gather
on the streets of Montgomery, May 1961.

On 30 May 1961, a group of seven men, under orders from General Juan Díaz, assassinated **Rafael Trujillo Senior**, the ruthless terrorist dictator of the Dominican Republic. An attempt to re-establish the Trujillo regime failed later in the year. (*Above*) The funeral of Trujillo, June 1961, and (*left*) Trujillo's death mask.

On 12 February 1961 news broke of the killing of **Patrice Lumumba**, Marxist Premier of the Congo, probably at the behest of Moise Tshombe, his Katangan rival. (*Left*) A protester at the UN building, New York. An even greater mystery hung over the death of the UN Secretary-General **Dag Hammarskjöld** (*Right*) in a plane crash in Northern Rhodesia on 18 September 1961. Many still believe this was the work of the CIA, MI5, and South African Intelligence.

The death of Lumumba brought no relief to the people of the Congo. The Katangan President **Moise Tshombe** (*right*) was briefly imprisoned but continued his fight to gain independence for Katanga. (*Above*) Katangan troops put members of the *Baluba Jeunesse* (Young Fighters) to flight outside the US Consulate, December 1961. The *Baluba Jeunesse* had previously been supporters of Lumumba.

Seven years after the departure of
the French, civil war still raged in
Vietnam. In the Cold War, US
strategy was to make a stand
against Communism wherever it
raised its ugly head, whether in the
US backyard, in the case of Cuba, or
on the other side of the world.

Early in the Kennedy administration, the decision was taken to send **US military advisers** to Vietnam to aid the South Vietnamese in their fight against the Communist North. (*Above*) South Vietnamese troops receive training in guerrilla warfare from US advisers. (*Left*) Vietnamese troops in training.

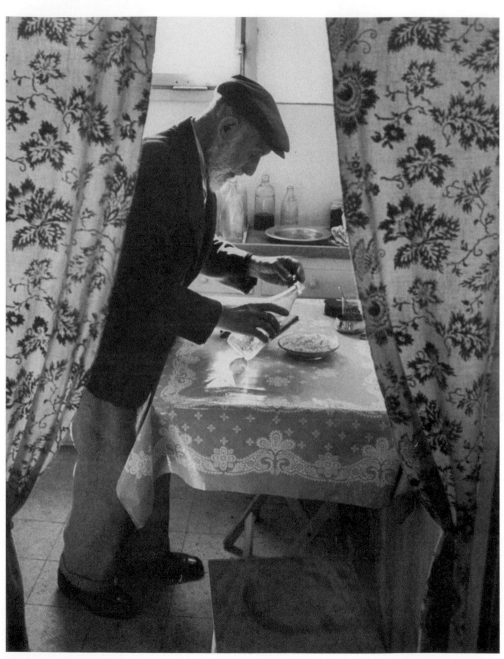

Adolf Eichmann, a man responsible for the deportation of thousands of Jews to concentration camps in World War II, escaped to Argentina in 1945. He was seized by Israeli agents in 1960, brought back to Israel, convicted of "crimes against humanity" and sentenced to death. (*Above*) Eichmann prepares his own defence, 12 April 1961. (*Left*) Mordehai Grynszpan, a Polish witness against Eichmann.

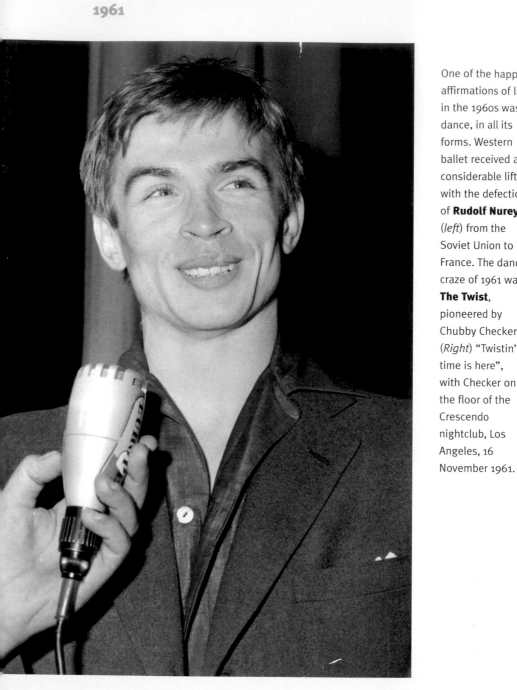

One of the happiest affirmations of life in the 1960s was dance, in all its forms. Western ballet received a considerable lift with the defection of **Rudolf Nureyev** (*left*) from the Soviet Union to France. The dance craze of 1961 was **The Twist**, pioneered by Chubby Checker. (*Right*) "Twistin' time is here", with Checker on the floor of the Crescendo nightclub, Los Angeles, 16 November 1961.

The cult art film of 1961 was Alain Resnais' *Last Year in Marienbad*. Box office smashes included *West Side Story* and Blake Edwards' **Breakfast at Tiffany's**, starring Audrey Hepburn. (*Left*) Hepburn in the black cocktail dress by Givenchy she wore in the film. A European hit was Fellini's **La Dolce Vita**. (*Right*) Marcello Mastroianni (on left) and Fellini pose by the film's poster.

Berlin was increasingly seen as the frontline flashpoint between East and West – with the western sector of the city a capitalist island in a sea of strict East German Communism. In fact, there were still four powers in the city: France, Britain, the US, and the USSR. Passage between the Soviet sector and the West was strictly regulated, but the desperate and the daring took their chances to cross from East to West. The Soviet response to this apparent threat to the East Germany economy was to build the Berlin Wall in October 1961. It was to last 28 years.

(*Right*) In the last summer before the Wall, young West Berliners chat with their grandparents in East Berlin. (*Above*) The Hammer-and-Sickle brigade turns to bricks and mortar to divide the city, October 1961.

1961   The Berlin Wall

The number of escapes increased. (*Left*) A woman leaves her apartment in Bernauer Strasse to make her way to Western freedom, 10 September 1961. (*Above*) US troops supervise Checkpoint Charlie, February 1961. Even after the Wall was built, this remained a legitimate point of passage between East and West Berlin. (*Right*) With the Wall, escape became riskier. West German police help a teenager to safety, October 1961.

The Wall was too high to jump, and barbed wire made climbing hazardous. (*Above*) A section of the Wall on Potsdamer Platz. (*Left*) An East German policeman inspects a gap in the Wall. Always guarded and constantly patrolled, the Wall still failed to deter would-be escapees. (*Right*) One that didn't get away... A barbed wire wreath decorates the cross on a memorial to one who died in a bid for freedom in August 1962.

Three years after training as an astronaut, Lieutenant Colonel **John Glenn** became the first American to orbit the earth. In his space voyage in the capsule *Friendship 7*, Glenn made three orbits during the Mercury-Atlas 6 Mission. (*Above*) Glenn boards the space capsule, 20 February 1962. (*Right*) On his return, Glenn rides in triumph with President Kennedy – his pioneer journey made him a national hero.

The **Algerian War of Independence** reached its bloody climax in 1962. At its peak, the French stationed 500,000 men in Algeria, but it wasn't enough. Two pictures from March 1962: (*left*) A dead man – possibly a member of the FLN, possibly a member of the OAS – lies on the streets of Algiers. (*Right*) A poster calling for "Peace in Algeria for our Children".

Fighting in Algeria ended with secret
peace talks at Evian-les-Bains in March
1962. Members of de Gaulle's
government and representatives of the
provisional government of Algeria, led
by Ben Bella, agreed a ceasefire and to
hold a **referendum** on independence.

The referendum received massive
support in both France and Algeria.
(*Left*) Algerian women queue to vote
in the referendum, 3 July 1962.
(*Above*) Crowds cheer **Mohammad
Ahmed Ben Bella**, founder of the FLN
and the new country's first President.

A life composed equally of pain and fame came to an end on 9 August 1962 with the **death of Marilyn Monroe**. She was just 36 years old. At first it was generally accepted that she had committed suicide – not until later did conspiracy theorists get to work. (*Left*) The room where she died. (*Above*) Headlines from two New York newspapers tell of her death – print this large was exceptional at this time.

The opposing cultures of freedom and oppression fought on in the southern states of the US. In September 1962, **James Meredith** (*above*) became the first African-American to be admitted to the University of Mississippi, though it took several US marshals to facilitate his entry. (*Left*) An effigy of Meredith hangs beneath the Confederate flag at the University.

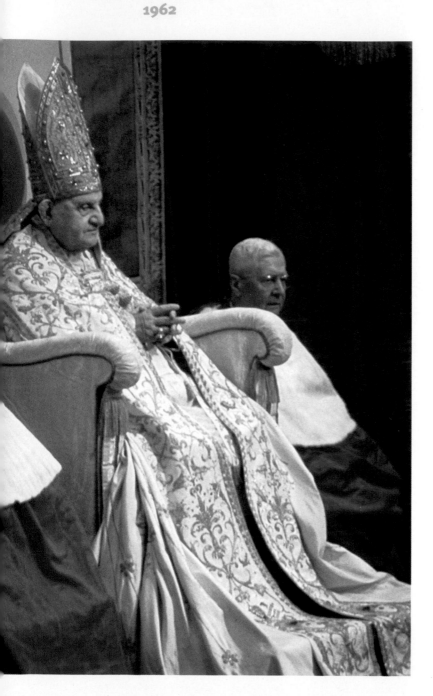

The Second Vatican **Ecumenical Council** of the Roman Catholic Church opened in St Peter's in October 1962 (*right*). It was convened by Pope John XXIII with the object of moving the Church forward and adapting to modern conditions. (*Left*) Pope John sits on the Papal Throne beneath the Bernini Canopy during the opening ceremony of the Council.

In October 1962, American surveillance
discovered that the USSR had established a
nuclear missile site in Cuba, and that missiles
were on their way across the Atlantic.
President Kennedy ordered an immediate
naval blockade of the island. (*Above*)
Americans gather in a TV store in Los Angeles
as the President announces the blockade.

The blockade intensified what became known as the **Cuban Missile Crisis**. Over the next few days, it seemed that nuclear war was inevitable. It was perhaps the most dramatic episode in the Cold War, with much of the world praying for peace. (*Above*) Members of the Campaign for Nuclear Disarmament march in London to protest against Kennedy's actions, 28 October 1962.

Fierce negotiations between Kennedy and the Soviet leader Nikita Krushchev resulted in the cargo ships carrying the **missiles** being recalled to the USSR – a decision that may well have saved the world. (*Left*) The Soviet freighter *Ivan Polzunov*, with missiles on board, is intercepted and turned back by the US Navy Picket ship *USS Vesole*, 10 November 1962.

In an uneasy world, other nations almost came to blows. Tension generated by cross-border incidents between **India and the People's Republic of China** threatened war late in 1962. (*Right*) Refugees from India's border territory arrive at Tezpur, 22 November. (*Left*) Members of the Indian Home Guard train in Tezpur during the crisis, 15 November.

Enter the brave... 1962 saw the first
appearance on screen of the suave and
multi-talented James Bond in **Dr No**.
The film was a huge success, enabling
(or condemning) Sean Connery to a
screen life composed of equal parts wine,
women, and danger for decades. (*Above*)
A misunderstanding between the CIA and
MI5 – Jack Lord pulls a gun on Connery.

The most spectacular film of 1962 was David Lean's **Lawrence of Arabia**, an uncritical biopic of the writer, warrior, mystic, and misfit T E Lawrence. The film won Oscars for Lean, his photographer Frederick A Young, and for Maurice Jarre's music. (*Above*) An encounter between Peter O'Toole as Lawrence (left) and Omar Sharif as Sheik Sherif Ali Ibn el Kharish.

Konrad Adenauer
was founder of
Germany's Christian
Democratic Union,
and Chancellor of
West Germany from
1949. In 1959 he
quarreled publicly
with his Finance
Minister, **Ludwig
Erhard**, who
succeeded him in
1963. (*Right*)
Adenauer points at
Erhard during a
Berlin CDU
reception marking
Adenauer's
resignation. (*Left*)
Erhard, with
customary cigar,
sits at the
Chancellor's desk,
September 1963.

One of the last acts of **Pope John XXIII** was to issue the encyclical *Pace in Terris* (Peace on Earth), advocating reconciliation between East and West. He died shortly after, mourned by Catholics and many others throughout the world. (*Right*) A double exposure image of John XXIII lying in state and Francesco Mochi's *Saint Veronica*, June 1963.

1963

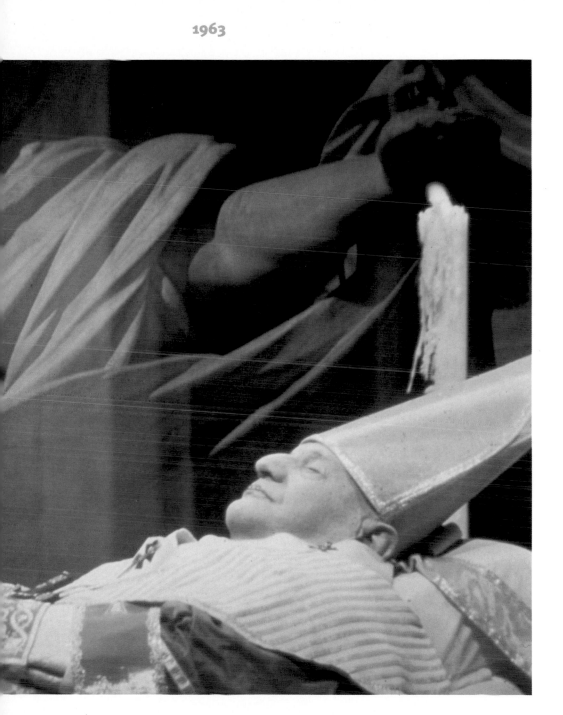

Valentina Tereshkova was an ex-cotton mill worker who joined the Soviet Cosmonaut Corps in 1962. She became a Hero of the State, pin-up and subject of a Soviet pop song after she became the first woman to orbit the earth. During her three-day voyage she was the solo pilot of the space capsule *Vostok 6*, returning to earth on 19 June 1963.

(*Left*) Tereshkova in her space suit shortly before launch from the Tyuratam Space Station... "Valya, my love, you are higher than even the Kremlin..." (*Above*) Crowds fill Red Square, Moscow to welcome Tereshkova on her return, and Valery Bykovsky, a Soviet cosmonaut who had spent more time in space than any other, 24 June 1963.

The **Profumo Affair** brought titillating shock and delight to the British press and public, and led to the Government's downfall. The key figures were Christine Keeler, a young call-girl (*left*); the Secretary of State for War, John Profumo (*above* – with his wife Valerie Hobson); and Eugene Ivanov, a Soviet navel attaché based in London...

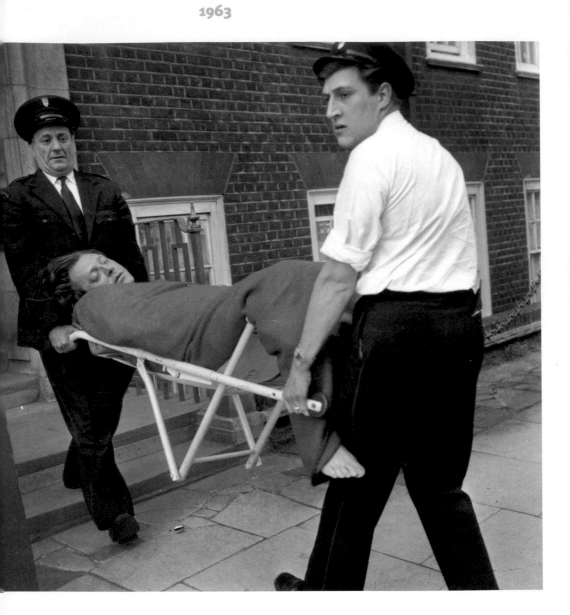

The fourth player was **Stephen Ward**, a society osteopath and
art dealer who introduced Keeler to Profumo. The Affair
exploded when Profumo lied to the House of Commons and
Ward was arrested and charged with living off immoral earnings.

Ward was found guilty but committed suicide before he could be sentenced. (*Left*) Ward is rushed to hospital, 31 July 1963. (*Above*) Keeler's colleague and fellow call-girl **Mandy Rice-Davies** at the launch of her biography *The Mandy Report*.

Berlin continued to be the focal point of East–West tension. On 27 October 1963, President Kennedy visited **West Berlin** and made a keynote speech acknowledging the importance he attached to the city. It became known as the "I am a Berliner" speech, although Kennedy's German was at fault. Instead of "Ich bin Berliner", he said "...ein Berliner", which translates as "I am a doughnut".

1963

The town of **Skopje** in Yugoslavia was badly damaged
in World War II. A generation later it was destroyed by an
earthquake that lasted three hours. Over 1,000 people
were killed and 170,000 were made homeless. (*Above*)
Troops and workers hunt for survivors, 26 July 1963.
(*Right*) A child sits in the rubble that was once her house.

On 8 August 1963, a gang halted the Glasgow–Euston Night Mail train, attacked the driver, and snatched 120 mailbags containing £2.5 million. The gang's audacity was matched by their carelessness, for they left fingerprints at a nearby remote farmhouse. (*Left*) The bridge at Sears Crossing where the **Great Train Robbery** took place. (*Above*) Eight days after the robbery, police escort gang members from Linslade Farm.

A crowning event of the Civil Rights Movement was the **March for Jobs and Freedom**. Over 200,000 people gathered in Washington DC to hear one of the finest orations of the 20th century. (*Right*) Some of the marchers crowd the open-air mall by the Washington Monument. (*Above*) Dr Martin Luther King addresses the marchers: "This will be the day when all of God's children will be able to sing... 'My country 'tis of thee, sweet land of liberty...'"

(*Left*) The Kennedys arrive at Love Field. (*Above*) The drive through downtown Dallas, seconds before the shooting: (left to right) JFK, Jacqueline Kennedy, Texas Governor John Connally, and his wife Nellie, 22 November 1963.

In less then two hours of violence, confusion, panic, and horror, the 35th President of the United States was assassinated on the streets of Dallas, and his successor was sworn in on board *Air Force One*. Nearly half a century later, the United States has barely recovered, with huge doubt still lingering as to who was responsible for the killing. The death of Kennedy was one of the time-stopping moments of the 20th century, a flash of fire in a Texan city that extinguished the flame of an administration that had promised great things for its citizens and the rest of the world.

(*Above*) New York commuters read of the death of their President.
(*Left*, *top*) In the hours when the facts seemed clear and certain...
Lee Harvey Oswald is taken into custody – two days later he was shot
by Jack Ruby. (*Left*, *below*) A Dallas detective holds up the Italian
Mannlicher-Carcano rifle with which Oswald allegedly shot Kennedy.

It all happened so quickly: the killing, flight back to Washington, post mortem, and funeral... (*Left*) Jacqueline Kennedy with her children John Jr and Caroline leaves the White House to attend the Lying-in-State, 26 November. (*Above*) Jacqueline Kennedy, flanked by her husband's brothers Edward (left) and Robert, joins in a nation's mourning.

It was the most expensive film ever made, at over four hours one of the longest, and it was slaughtered by the critics. Its star described Joseph Mankiewicz's **Cleopatra** as "...the most bizarre piece of entertainment ever..." (*Left*) Elizabeth Taylor as Cleopatra (back to camera, foreground) surveys her people. (*Right*) Rex Harrison as Caesar with Taylor in a highly political moment from the film.

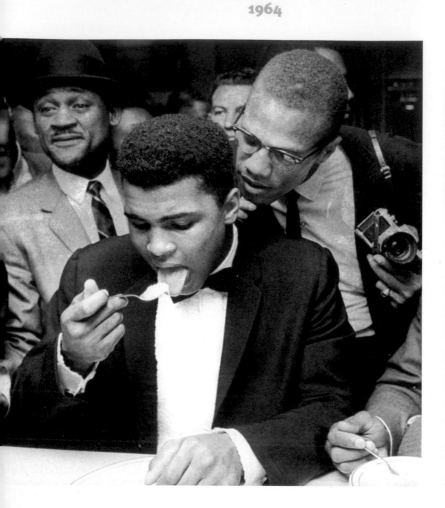

On 25 February 1964 **Cassius Clay** took the
World Heavyweight Boxing title when he defeated
Sonny Liston in Miami. (*Right*) Clay declares "I am
the greatest..." as his seconds rush to hug him
at his moment of triumph. (*Above*) Malcolm X has
a word in Clay's ear. Perhaps the seeds of Clay's
name change to Muhammad Ali were being sown.

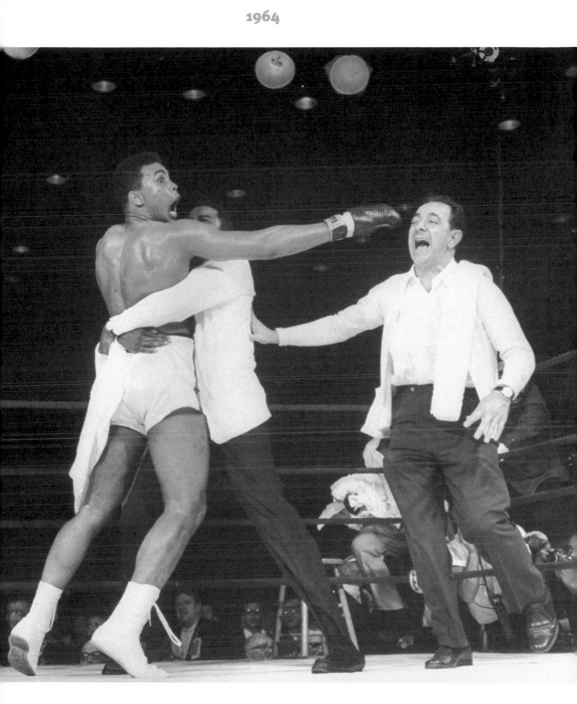

The **New York World's Fair** of 1964 (*above*) was billed as the Space Age Fair, a Universal and International exposition with the theme of "Peace Through Understanding". It occupied almost a square mile and attracted 51 million visitors. Its centrepiece was the giant stainless steel *Unisphere* (*left*).

A year earlier, Martin Luther King had described Mississippi as a state "sweltering in injustice". In June 1964 three **civil rights workers** disappeared. Their bodies were found weeks later in Neshoba County, Mississippi. (*Above*) The burnt-out station wagon in which the three young men were last seen alive. (*Right*) Protestors at the Democratic National Convention, August 1964, hold posters of the victims – (left to right) Andrew Goodman, James Chaney, and Michael Schwerner.

After 13 years in opposition, the Labour
Party gained power in the 1964 British
General Election, promoting the image of
being more in touch with modern times.
(*Above*) Labour leader **Harold Wilson**
chats with The Beatles at a Show Business
Awards ceremony, London, 19 March 1964.
(*Left*) Wilson campaigns in Wales.

The incumbent Democrat Lyndon Johnson and the Republican candidate Barry Goldwater fought the 1964 **US Presidential election**. (*Left*) Goldwater on the campaign trail in Santa Barbara, California. (*Right*) Johnson and Vice-President Hubert Humphrey (on right) celebrate their November victory with plates of ribs in Austin, Texas.

The fashion war of the 1960s was between
Mods (neat dress/Italian scooters) and
Rockers (leather gear/roaring bikes) in
Britain. Much of the rivalry was good-natured
(*above*), but pitched battles occurred in
seaside towns. (*Left*) **Mods and Rockers**
fight in Hastings, 3 August 1964. (*Below*)
A beach-head battle at Margate, 18 May.

It was the first golden age of the young **style gurus**, rapidly rising to fame through the medium of *boutique* or *salon*. (*Left*) John Stephen, outside his The Mod Male shop, catering for the suit-and-scooter clientele, July 1964. (*Above*) Two of the biggest names in Swinging London fashion... Vidal Sassoon gives Mary Quant a cut, 18 November.

Beatlemania

No phenomenon better marks the pre-eminence of youth in the Sixties than the rise of The Beatles. In less than four years the Fab Four went from a club in Hamburg to a worldwide audience, backed by their manager Brian Epstein and their Record Manager George Martin. First there was *Please Please Me*, then *A Hard Days' Night*, *Revolver*, *Sergeant Pepper*, and on and on... Beatlemania gripped their tearful and jubilant young fans. Older admirers wrote essays analysing The Beatles's success. And, as the Sixties unrolled, John, Paul, George, and Ringo became bigger and bigger, until it seemed they would go on for ever.

(*Left*) The Fab Four at a press conference in San Francisco, August 1964. (*Above*) The Trembling Two... fans await the arrival of the group at New York, 10 February 1964.

Wherever they went, The Beatles attracted immense crowds whose enthusiasm often crossed the border into hysteria. Never one to miss an opportunity to move from cheek to bad taste, Lennon once joked that they were "more popular than Jesus". Certainly, they were more popular than anyone else on earth. (*Left*) Police hold back the worshippers outside the London Pavilion for the premiere of *A Hard Day's Night*, 7 July 1964. (*Above*) A still from the film, directed by Richard Lester: (left to right) Paul, George, Ringo, and John.

Almost at the crest of the wave... The Beatles invade the States early in 1964. (*Right*) Boarding their flight from London Heathrow, 7 February 1964. (*Left*) Forty-eight hours later – with their TV-show host Ed Sullivan, New York, 9 February. (*Above*) Another day in the life... The Beatles at the Washington Coliseum, 13 February.

The nearest British rivals to The Beatles were the raunchier **Rolling Stones**. (*Right*) The Stones in Hanover Square, London: (left to right) Mick Jagger, Keith Richards, Bill Wyman, Brian Jones, and Charlie Watts. (*Above*) In the US the big band was **The Beach Boys**: (left to right) Carl Wilson, Brian Wilson, Mike Love, Al Jardine, and Dennis Wilson.

The other great sound of the Sixties was Motown. (*Left*) **The Supremes** in October 1964: (left to right) Mary Wilson, Diana Ross, and Florence Ballard in the days of *Baby Love*. (*Above*) **Motown** founder Berry Gordy plays piano at the Motown Studios – among those hanging around are Smokey Robinson (background) and a young Stevie Wonder (second from right).

The 1964 Olympic Games were held in Tokyo. One of the stars of the Games was the New Zealand athlete **Peter Snell**, who became the first runner since the 1920 Games in Antwerp to win gold in both the Men's 800 and 1,500 Metres. (*Right*) The 1,500 Metre Final – Snell is 466, fellow New Zealander John Davies (467) won bronze.

(*Left*) **Sheila Matthews** waves to the crowd after husband **Ken**'s victory for Britain in the 20 Kilometre Walk. She had just given him the longest kiss in Olympic history. (*Above*) **Valery Brumel** of the USSR sets a new Olympic record of 2.18 metres in the High Jump, 21 October 1964. (*Right*) Swedish cyclist **Gösta Petterson** takes on supplies during the Road Race, 23 October.

The Bond film of 1964 was **Goldfinger**, in which gold-painted Shirley Eaton (*right*) perished lamentably early on. A character who could well have been a Bond villain was Dr Strangelove (*left*), played by Peter Sellers in **Dr Strangelove or: How I Learned to Stop Worrying and Love the Bomb**.

1964

1965

Sixty days after receiving the Nobel Peace prize, Martin Luther King Jr was in jail in Selma, Alabama. With others, he was organizing a march from **Selma to Montgomery**, to affirm black voting rights. Two attempts to march were beaten back. (*Above*) The marchers set out at last on 21 March 1965. (*Left*) Law enforcement officers guard the Capitol Building in Montgomery, 25 March.

There was violent white opposition to the march, some of the worst coming from local police. One of King's supporters, a Unitarian Minister named **James Reeb**, was beaten to death in Selma. (*Left*) A woman protester is arrested outside the White House. (*Right*) A massive demonstration in Los Angeles, also in protest at Reeb's death, March 1965.

The Space Race took a step forward with the **first spacewalks** by cosmonauts from the USSR and the USA. (*Above*) Alexei Leonov on board *Voskhod 2*, from which he took the first walk in space, 18 March 1965. (*Right*) Edward White, the first American to walk in space, 160 kilometres (100 miles) above earth, 3 June 1965.

Eight years after work was started, the
Mont Blanc Tunnel was completed in July
1965. Connecting Chamonix, France with
Courmayeur, Italy, the 11.6-kilometre (seven-
mile) long and 8.6-metre (28-feet) wide
tunnel passed beneath the highest mountain
in Europe. It was the longest in the world.

(*Left*) One of the telephone points, equipped with fire extinguishers and sited every 300 metres (984 feet) throughout the tunnel's length. (*Above*) The **motor cavalcade** carrying Italian President Giuseppe Saragat and party passes through the tunnel, 19 July 1965.

In August 1965 racial violence exploded in the predominately black district of **Watts**, Los Angeles. Thirty people were killed, hundreds injured and 2,000 arrested in rioting and looting that lasted five days. (*Left*) Some of the 20,000 national guardsmen drafted into Watts between 10 and 15 August.

Violence spread rapidly, and the
Governor of California, Edmund
"Pat" Brown, was forced to call in
Federal troops and impose a curfew
before order was restored. (*Above*)
A **national guardsman** stands in
rubble outside a looted shop.

But clampdown wasn't enough.
President Johnson declared:
"We must strike at the unjust
conditions from which disorder
largely flows". (*Above*) Armed
police stand over alleged
rioters on the streets of Watts.

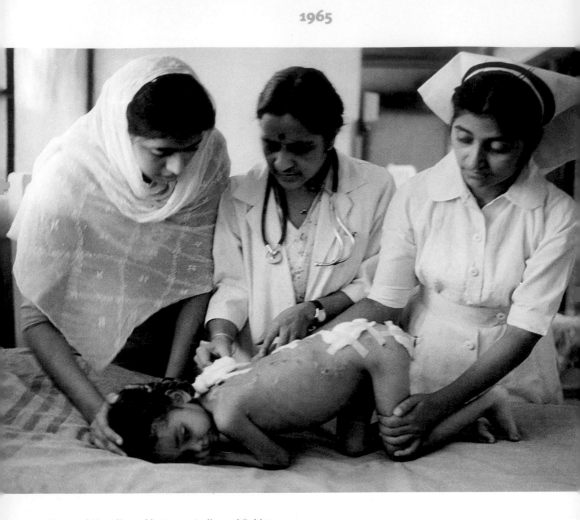

The rumbling discord between India and Pakistan
erupted in August 1965, when what became known
as the **Second Kashmir War** broke out. Kashmir had
remained a disputed area ever since the partition
of India in 1947. On 15 August, Indian troops (*right*)
marched into the province and full scale fighting
erupted. (*Above*) A child injured in a bombing raid is
treated in a Punjabi hospital, 17 September 1965.

Following the disappearance of several children, police conducted a massive hunt in what became known as the **Moors Murders**. (*Left*) Volunteers comb moorland between Manchester and Sheffield, 25 November 1965. The killers were Ian Brady and Myra Hindley, a couple who became the most hated people in Britain. (*Right*) Ten-year-old Lesley Ann Downey, one of their victims.

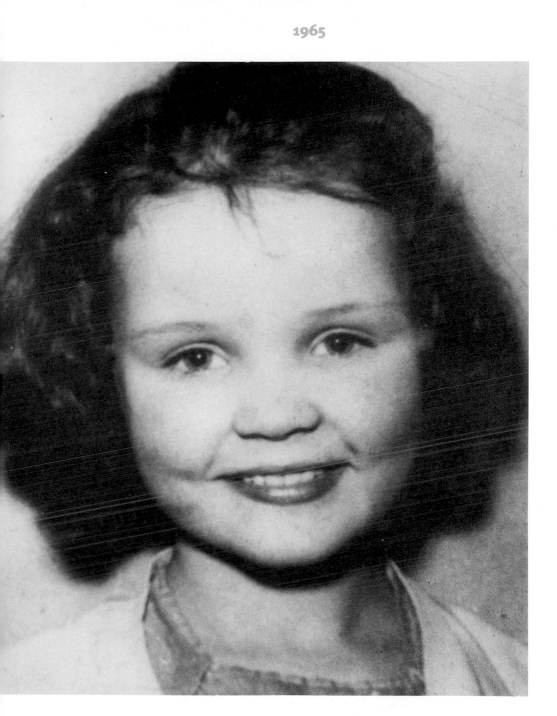

By the autumn of 1965 the US military had already lost 650 men in **Vietnam**. There was mounting discontent at home. Standards of fitness for recruits were lowered. Draft cards were burnt in increasing numbers. President Johnson bit deeper into the bullet, raising the total number of troops in Vietnam to 108,000. (*Left*) Men of the 7th US Marines wade ashore at Cape Batangan, November 1965.

The killing now rapidly escalated. On 20 September 1965, seven US planes were downed in one day. Civilian deaths increased. Permission was given to use teargas. On 30 October US jets bombed a friendly village, killing 48 inhabitants. (*Left*) A **Viet Cong** prisoner, taken during the new offensive. (*Above*) A **US Marine** carries a wounded Vietnamese child.

The nightmare intensified. In November 1965, 240 US troops died in a single week. (*Above*) Terrified **Vietnamese civilians** flee from conflict between US troops and members of the Viet Cong, Cape Batangan. (*Right*) US **napalm** bombs explode in fields south of Saigon.

At 05.17 on the evening of 9 November 1965, a power switch failed at an electricity station near Niagara Falls. The result was a **power failure** that affected nine US states and parts of Canada. Motorists (*above*) were not amused.

Most of the 23 million people plunged into darkness accepted their fate with good humour, however, and nine months later there was a surge in the birthrate. (*Above*) Passengers make their way on foot along a subway tunnel during the **blackout**.

Writers, artists, and performers all became
involved in the rising Western culture of
protest. Folk singers took the lead, among
them (*left*) **Bob Dylan** and **Joan Baez**.
Dylan's *The Times They Are a-Changin'*
became an anthem of protest. (*Above*) Writer
Norman Mailer, author of *An American
Dream* and later *Why Are We In Vietnam?*, at
home with his son Michael and wife Beverly.

The two most successful films of 1965 both took
as their theme a hero's resistance to political
repression. For David Lean (*left*, directing
Julie Christie) the text was Boris Pasternak's
Dr Zhivago. For Robert Wise (*above*, standing
with Christopher Plummer and Julie Andrews)
the theme was underscored by Rodgers
and Hammerstein's **The Sound of Music**.

James Meredith, a reluctant hero from the campaign to integrate "Ol' Miss", began the **March Against Fear**, on his own, from Memphis, Tennessee to Jackson, Mississippi in June 1966. His object was to encourage black Americans to register and vote, but at the very beginning, he was hit by a shotgun blast. Others marched for him (*left*), including (*above*, left to right) Floyd B McKissick, Martin Luther King, and Stokely Carmichael.

Wearing the smile that had carried him through many Hollywood B list films, **Ronald Reagan** made his first bid for public office in September 1966. In the gubernatorial elections in California, Ronnie the Republican (*above*, on horseback) defeated the incumbent Edmund G "Pat" Brown. (*Right*) Reagan and Nancy at the victory party.

In 1966 73-year-old **Mao Zedong** was engaged in a power struggle with his former comrades Lin Piao and Deng Xiaoping. It was important to Mao's cause that he appear still strong enough to lead his people, hence these retouched photos of Mao swimming the Yangtze (*left*), and emerging triumphant from the waters (*above*), 16 July 1966.

What followed was the **Cultural Revolution**, a ruthless review of the machinery of government and its operators in contemporary China. (*Left*) A young member of the pro-Mao Red Guard pins an armband on her beloved leader Mao Zedong, 8 September 1966. (*Above*) Red Guards chant in unison as they read Mao's *Little Red Book*.

Roger Hunt of England raises his arms as the West German goalkeeper Hans Tilkowski fails to grab the ball. The ball hit the crossbar and thudded back almost on the goal-line. The Russian linesman judged that it had crossed the line. Contemporary opinion believes it didn't. Nevertheless, it was England's crucial third goal in the **World Cup Final**, Wembley, 30 July 1966.

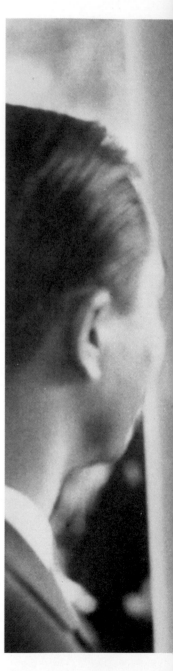

The **war in Vietnam** polarized opinion across the world.
Lyndon B Johnson brooded on the cost in dollars and
lives, but still backed the South Vietnamese regime.
(*Right*) Johnson meets the Premier Cao Ky Nguyen.
(*Above*) Philippine students demonstrate against the
war, Manila, October 1966. At the time, Johnson was
paying a surprise visit to US troops in Vietnam.

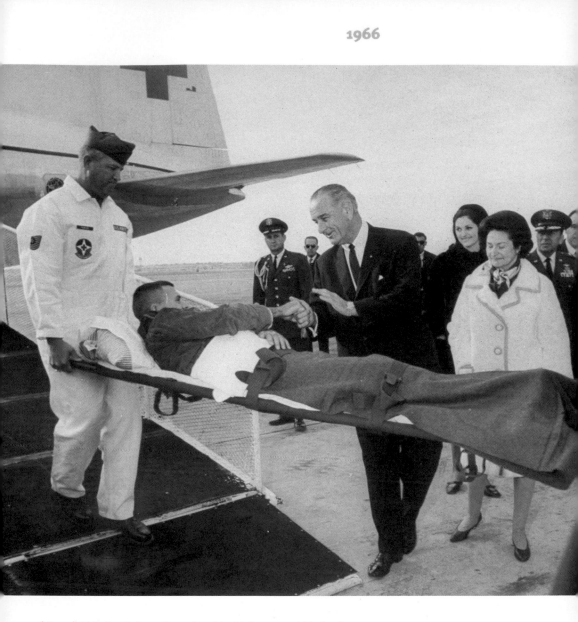

(*Above*) At Kelly Air Force Base, President Johnson and his family greet **wounded US servicemen** returning from Vietnam, December 1966. Two months earlier, in Bangkok, he had told his troops to come home "safe and sound". (*Right*) An **anti-war demonstrator** at a session of the HUAC, Washington DC, 17 August 1966.

At 09.30 on 21 October 1966
a slag heap slithered into the
Welsh village of **Aberfan** (*left*),
burying the Pantglas Junior
School and killing 190 people,
most of them children. The slag
had been built over a spring, and
heavy rain created an avalanche
of mud. (*Above*) Families attend
a mass funeral, 28 October 1966.

On 4 November 1966 the River Arno burst its
banks, **flooding the city of Florence**, killing 100
people, and damaging buildings and works of
art. (*Above*) The flooded museum of Accademia,
with Michaelangelo's *David* in the background.
(*Right*) One of the hundreds of damaged
paintings is carried through flooded streets.

Glitterati at the 1966 **Cannes Film Festival**. (*Clockwise from bottom left*) Members of the Festival Jury that presented top film awards to *Un Homme et Une Femme* and *Signore e Signori*, (left to right) Armand Salacrou, Marcel Achard, Maurice Genevoix, Andre Maurois, Tetsuro Furukaki; Catherine Deneuve and her husband, the English photographer David Bailey; Raquel Welch; and Monica Vitti.

(*Above*) Ossie Clark (second from left) and Neil Winterbottom (far left) pose in front of Albert Little's *Swinging Sixties* etching. (*Right*) A 1960s bold print scarf and beach dress.

The rag trade and the music business brought glory to London. The places to be were Carnaby Street and the King's Road, Chelsea. Male and female fashion was ablaze with style and colour. Mini-skirted chicks and sharply-tailored guys strutted their way round Knightsbridge and Kensington. The pill liberated an entire generation of young men and women. Love was all you needed. Britannia ruled the musical airwaves. Drugs were the new fish and chips. Everyone, but *everyone*, darling, party-ed till dawn. It was the Swinging Sixties.

The Swinging Sixties   1966

The Sixties fashion revolution presented materials both new and traditional in bold new styles. (*Left*) A French model poses in a knitted coat faced with leather patches by Paco Rabanne. (*Above*) Ready-to-wear skimpy jumpers and pleated skirts – the model on the right is Lesley Hornby, better known as Twiggy, an icon of the Swinging Sixties.

The essence of the Sixties look. (*Above*) A young customer tries on a hat at the Biba boutique in Kensington, July 1966. (*Right*) Twiggy bedecked in Sixties make-up, baggy fur coat, and exquisite retro-Twenties style hat, November 1966. (*Far right*) Alan Fitch, proprietor of the *I Was Lord Kitchener's Valet* boutique in West London's Portobello Road, December 1966.

One film that captured the spirit of the
Swinging Sixties was based on Bill
Naughton's play **Alfie**. (*Above*) Michael
Caine and Shirley Anne Field in a
scene that captures the essence of the
film. (*Right*) Sean Connery as 007 is
sponged down in **You Only Live Twice**,
the most expensive Bond film to date.

One of the most popular TV series of 1966 was **Batman**, an enjoyably "camp" treatment that managed to maintain a good deal of the old Marvel Comics style. (*Left*) Adam West as Batman, with one of his arch-enemies, (*right*) Catwoman played by Julie Newmar, an earlier star of *Seven Brides for Seven Brothers*.

On 5 January 1967, millions of TV viewers watched in horror as **Donald Campbell's** attempt to break his own water-speed record of 432.66 kph (276.33 mph) ended in tragedy. As his turbojet hydroplane *Bluebird* approached 470 kph (300 mph) on Coniston Water in Cumbria, the nose lifted from the water (*above*), and the hydroplane performed a backwards somersault (*left, from left to right*). Campbell was killed.

On 18 March 1967, the 277-metre (975-foot) tanker **Torrey Canyon**, carrying 117,000 tons of oil, ran aground on the Seven Stones Reef near Land's End. In an attempt to limit the oil slick's damage to the Cornish coast, the RAF dropped high explosives and napalm on the wreck, but over 160 kilometres (100 miles) of beach and coastline were already contaminated.

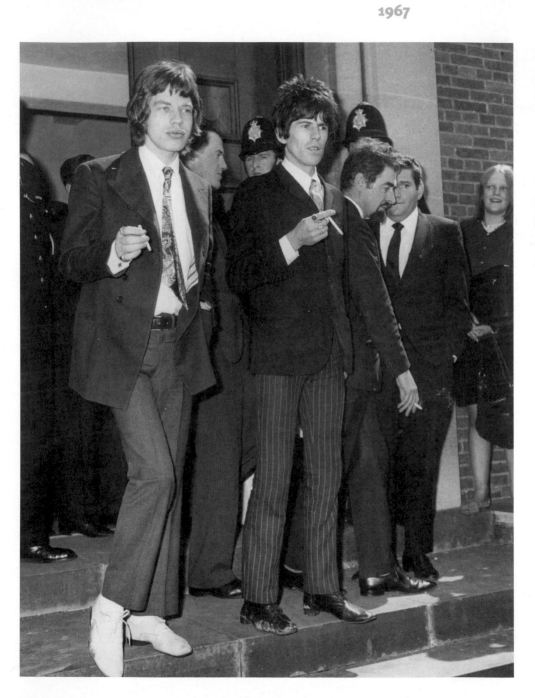

A *cause célèbre* of the Swinging Sixties in 1967 was the arrest and brief imprisonment of two members of **The Rolling Stones** for smoking dope. (*Left*) Mick Jagger and Keith Richards outside Chichester Magistrates Court, 10 May. (*Above*) Paul McCartney (centre) and Jane Asher show their support for The Stones.

It became known as the **Six Day War**, a lightning
strike by Israeli troops against Egypt, Syria, and
Jordan following an Egyptian advance into the
Sinai Desert. Within a week, the Israelis had
occupied Sinai, the Gaza Strip, and Old Jerusalem.
(*Above*) On the first day of the war, 5 June, Israeli
soldiers guard Egyptian prisoners in Rafah.
(*Right*) Israeli Prime Minister David Ben-Gurion
visits the Wailing Wall in Jerusalem, 12 June.

Although not the only US city to be hit by civil unrest in the summer of 1967, the **riots in Detroit** were the most violent, with dozens of people killed. Mayor Jerome P Cavanagh described his city as resembling Berlin in 1945. (*Above*) Police parade sniper suspects in an apartment building. (*Right*) National guardsmen patrol the streets, July 1967.

The last of the great Cunard transatlantic liners was launched at the John Brown shipyards on the Clyde on 20 September 1967. The 65,863 ton Queen Elizabeth II, better known as the **QE2**, cost £25.5 million to build. (*Left*) One of the ship's twin screw propellers. (*Right*) A seagull's eye view of the ship's launching by Queen Elizabeth.

In 1965 the Argentinian **Ernesto Che Guevara** left Cuba for an unknown destination. By 1967 he had joined forces seeking to overthrow the regime in Bolivia. On 8 October he was captured by government troops. One day later he was shot and his body placed on display for a press conference (*above*).

It was a blow to the cause of revolution throughout Central and South America. For **Fidel Castro** it was also a personal blow, the loss of a friend and companion. (*Above*) Castro holds up a photograph that shows General Ovando Candia and other members of the Bolivian Army Command celebrating the death of Guevara.

The King's wedding... (*Above*) **Elvis Presley** and Priscilla
Beaulieu, cut their cake at the Aladdin Hotel, Las Vegas,
2 May 1967. At the reception, 100 guests dined on
ham, Eggs Minette, Southern fried chicken, Oysters
Rockefeller, and candied salmon. (*Right*) The Shah's
coronation... **Mohammad Reza** (left) with his son and
the Shahbanou, Queen Farah, 26 October 1967.

It was a year when top film actresses landed feisty roles. (*Above*) Faye Dunaway as **Bonnie Parker**, (*left*) Jane Fonda as **Barbarella**, and (*right*) Elizabeth Taylor as **Katharina** in Zeffirelli's *The Taming of the Shrew*.

Vietnam 1968

By 1968 the strain on men, morale, and resources in the Vietnam war was immense. The two years from 1966 had seen the number of US troops in Vietnam increased from 184,000 to 537,000. The average monthly toll of US lives had risen from 172 in 1965 to 1,200 in 1968. President Johnson's attempts to ignore both Doves and Hawks, and pursue a middle-of-the-road war of attrition, was proving a nightmare abroad and a disaster at home. Early in 1968 came the Communist Tet (New Year) offensive, a sweeping attack on 100 cities, including Saigon. The writing was on the wall.

(*Left*) A tank is used as a makeshift ambulance to convey wounded US Marines during the battle to recapture Hue, January 1968. (*Above*) A widow grieves over the remains of her husband, found in a mass grave, February 1968.

215

In March a major assault by US and
South Vietnamese troops on the
ancient city of Hue resulted in massive
destruction. (*Above*) One of Hue's
avenues after a raid by US B-52
bombers. (*Right*) A Chinese-born
shopkeeper surveys the wreckage of
his home, 13 March. (*Left*) Refugees
return to the city. Johnson sent another
10,500 combat troops from the US.

On 16 March 1968 troops rounded up the inhabitants of the village of My Lai (*left*). The complete truth as to what happened will never be known. Houses were set on fire by US soldiers (*above*), and civilian women and children were massacred (*right*). The man held responsible was Lieutenant William Calley Jr, who was later court martialled and sentenced to 21 years imprisonment.

In the early spring of 1968, **Dr Martin Luther King Jr** was busy co-ordinating the Civil Rights Movement's "Poor People's Campaign" across the US. While working in Memphis, Tennessee, he was shot and killed at the Lorraine Hotel on 4 April. (*Right*) Dr Ralph Abernathy, Jesse Jackson, and others indicate where the shots came from. (*Above*) James Earl Ray, accused of the killing, swears he is innocent before the House Committee Investigation of Assassinations.

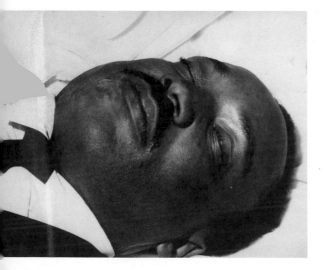

(*Right*) The **funeral of Dr Martin Luther King**, 8 April 1968. King's widow, Coretta Scott King, is in the centre of the front row of mourners, with King's great friend and colleague, Dr Ralph Abernathy, on her left. Harry Belafonte is with King's children, on the left of the picture. (*Above*) The man who sought to redeem the "soul of America" – Martin Luther King at rest.

On 2 May 1968, the administration shut down the
Sorbonne, the university in the heart of **Paris**, locking
out the students. Four days later, 20,000 students,
teachers, and supporters marched on the Sorbonne.
It was the first move in what became a near
revolution fought out on the streets of Paris. Trains
stopped running. Airports closed. Mail and telephone
communications were cut. Barricades were erected.

By 14 May 1968, after calls by labour unions for a general strike, Paris was a battleground. (*Left*) Riot police, with tear-gas guns at the ready, prepare to take on demonstrators. It was not long before police brutality fuelled further demonstrations. (*Above*) With over a million people on the streets, students from the **Sorbonne** join workers in running battles with the police and CRS.

The Sorbonne was re-opened by the authorities, and was promptly occupied by students and declared an "autonomous People's University". (*Above*) One of the student leaders and a key figure in the events of May '68, **Daniel Cohn-Bendit**, aka "Danny the Red". De Gaulle stood firm, delivering a speech that François Mitterand condemned as "a call to civil war". (*Right*) A mass demonstration against the Gaullist regime, 7 June 1968. The crisis ended with a whimper later that month.

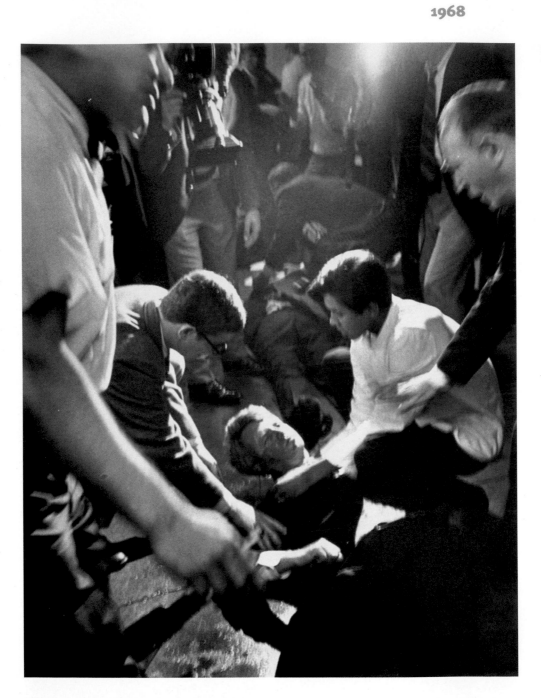

At 00.15 on 5 June 1968, shortly after winning the California Primary in his Presidential campaign, **Bobby Kennedy** was shot by Sirhan Sirhan at the Ambassador Hotel, Los Angeles. (*Right*) Busboy Juan Romero attempts to lift Kennedy's head. (*Left*) Reporters and camera crews gather round the wounded Kennedy. (*Above*, *left*) Kennedy wife Ethel gazes at her husband, then (*Above*, *right*) turns to beseech members of the media to move away. Kennedy died 26 hours later.

A disastrous famine in West African led to the province
of **Biafra** seceding from Federal Nigeria in 1967. In the
bitter civil war that followed, millions died from hunger,
thousands more were killed. (*Right*) A starving child in a
Nigerian refugee camp, 12 July 1968. (*Above*) A Federal
soldier threateningly guards women and children prisoners.

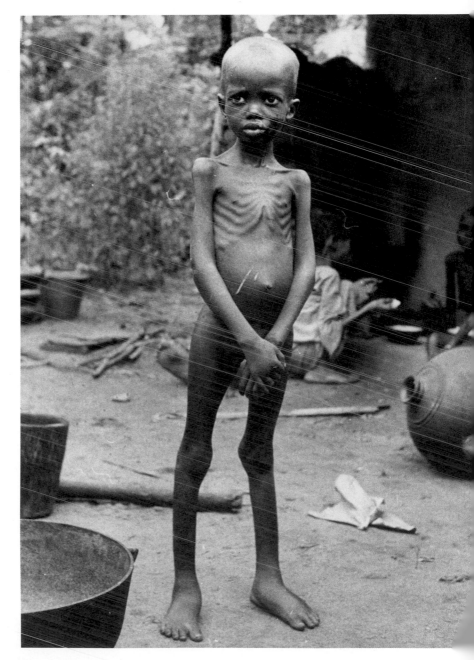

As in Hungary in 1956, so in Czechoslovakia in 1968. The **Prague Spring** was an attempt at liberalization and reform by Communist leader Alexander Dubcek. Once again Soviet reaction was swift and brutal. (*Left*) Prague citizens carrying Czech national flags take on Soviet tanks, 21 August 1968. (*Above*) Dead and wounded are removed from the cobbled streets. Within weeks the Prague Spring was over, crushed by the might of Warsaw Pact troops.

The **Mexico City Olympic Games** were a triumph for US athletes, who won 106 medals between them. Bob Beamon (*left*) set a new World Record in the Men's Long Jump, despite having sex with his wife the night before. But the games are remembered for the presentation of medals for the Men's 200 Metres (*right*), when Tommie Smith (centre) and John Carlos gave the Black Power salute.

The theatre sensation of 1968
was the Tribal Rock Musical
Hair (*above*), with peace, love,
and nudity flowering onstage.
(*Right*) Keir Dullea in futuristic
danger in the Stanley Kubrick
film **2001: A Space Odyssey**.

Just over a year late, the world's first supersonic jet airliner took off from Toulouse Airport for a 30 minute maiden flight on 2 March 1969. Another seven months passed before **Concorde**'s first supersonic flight. (*Above*) Air stewardesses working on *Concorde* for different airlines parade before a scale model. (*Left*) French make-up and accessories styled *à la Concorde*.

Just under a year after the riots of May '68,
French President **Charles de Gaulle** at last
relinquished power, following the defeat of his
referendum proposals for senate and regional
reforms. His truculence remained intact. (*Above*)
His glory days behind him, de Gaulle casts his
vote in the referendum, 27 April 1969.

De Gaulle's successor was **Georges Pompidou**, de Gaulle's former Prime Minister, and a man whose policies had done much to circumvent revolution in 1968. Many suspected de Gaulle dismissed Pompidou through jealousy of his success. (*Above*) Pompidou (standing) rides along the Champs Elysees following his investiture as President, 20 June 1969.

The Hippy Hippy Shake rocked and rolled ever onwards to the end of the 1960s and beyond. **John Lennon** and **Yoko Ono** spent seven days in bed in the Presidential Suite at the Amsterdam Hilton (*left*), protesting against "war and violence in the world", March 1969.
The Stones simply went on roaring. (*Above*) Marianne Faithfull (behind photographers) peers up as Mick Jagger lets rip at the free **Hyde Park Concert**, 5 July 1969.

The dream had existed for centuries: the great day came at last. On 16 July 1969, the spaceship **Apollo 11** lifted off from Cape Kennedy (*left*), carrying Neil Armstrong, Buzz Aldrin, and Michael Collins. Four days, six hours, and 45 minutes later, one fifth of the world's population watched on TV as Aldrin followed in Armstrong's "giant leap" footsteps on the Moon's Sea of Tranquility (*right*).

The three astronauts spent just over 21 hours on the Moon before returning to earth and splashing down just 24 km (15 miles) from their recovery ship *USS Hornet*. (*Above*, left to right) Armstrong, Collins, and Aldrin are visited in their **Mobile Quarantine Facility** by President Richard Nixon, 24 July 1969.

It had been a tremendous triumph for the States. They had overtaken the Russians in the space race, and the Stars and Stripes had been the first flag to fly on the Moon. The astronauts received a suitable hero's welcome at their **Ticker-Tape Parade** in New York City, 21 August 1969.

In the early hours of 9 August 1969 members of **Charles Manson**'s "Family" entered Roman Polanski's Beverly Hills home, killing five people, including Polanski's pregnant wife, actress Sharon Tate (*right*, with Polanski). (*Above*) Polanski on the bloodstained porch of his home the following day. (*Far right*) Manson at an early court hearing.

On 12 August 1969 the Protestant Apprentice Boys marched into the Catholic Bogside area of Derry, Northern Ireland. Over 1,000 people were injured in the three days of fighting that followed. (*Above*) Members of the RUC prepare for trouble 13 August 1969. (*Right*) **Bernadette Devlin**, Independent Unity MP for Mid Ulster and the youngest MP in Parliament, was later convicted of "incitement to riot" in the **Battle of the Bogside**.

(*Left*) Members of the **Royal Ulster Constabulary** fire tear-gas cartridges on the first day of the fighting. They were poorly equipped, with small riot shields and uniforms that were not flame resistant, and though they had guns and armoured vehicles, they were not allowed to use them. They also had to fight for three days and nights without relief or rest.

Billed by its young promoters as "Three Days of Peace and Music",
Woodstock attracted 450,000 fans to a pasture in Sullivan County
between 15 and 18 August 1969. The Jefferson Airplane, Creedence
Clearwater Revival and The Who signed for double their usual fees.
Hendrix came for $32,000. The Festival was such a success, it needed
a whole raft of new state laws to ensure it would never happen again.

Index *Page numbers refer to text references*